CELEBRITY PASTA DISHES

Created by **ASK** in aid of Great Ormond Street Hospital Children's Charity

40 MOUTH-WATERING PASTA RECIPES   Foreword by Vernon Kay and Tess Daly. Edited by Alon Shulman.

Published by World Famous Books
A division of World Famous Group.

WFG 35A Huntsworth Mews,
London NW1 6DB
www.worldfamousgroup.com

Logo © 2007 Great Ormond Street Hospital Children's
Charity Registered Charity Number 235825

Logo © 2009 ASK Restaurants Limited

Facts and excerpts from 'A Mess of Iguanas, A Whoop of Gorillas...
An Amazement of Animal Facts' by Alon Shulman used with
permission.

The right of Alon Shulman to be identified as the author of this work has been asserted by
him in accordance with the Copyright, Designs and Patent Act 1988.

The publisher thanks the following for their special contribution to
this book; Emma English at ASK Restaurants, Emma Bibizadeh and
Simon Kaston at Great Ormond Street Hospital Children's Charity,
World Famous Group, James Saville, Simon Smith Photography,
Antonio Vinciguerra, Samantha West, Lesley Davey and Sophie Hicks.

Project Concept &	Alon Shulman
Contributor/Celebrity Sourcing:	alon@worldfamousgroup.com
Food Photography:	Toby Scott
Food Stylist & Recipe Co-ordinator:	Mari Mererid Williams
ASK Marketing & Brand Ambassador:	Sharon David
Book Design:	The Core
Design Consultant:	Fresh Lemon
WFG Print Manager:	Martin Roach

Photo Credits:
Vivienne Westwood by Christian Shambanait
Simon Schama by Margherita Mirabella
Sir Ranulph Fiennes by www.ianparnell.com,
Zoë Wanamaker by Neil Genower
Gregg Wallace by Des Willie
Michael Palin by John Swannell
Ronni Ancona by Sven Arnstein/Stay Still/Photoshot
Pattie Boyd by Lesley G. Aggar
Claudia Winkleman by Simon Songhurst.
Nicki Chapman by Steve Schofield
Chesney Hawkes by Nevel James
Stephen Merchant by Carolyn Djanogly
Martin Freeman by Nicky Johnston, Camera Press London
Sir Chris Bonington by Roger Scruton, Chris Bonington Picture Library
Hugh Quarshie by John Falzon
Robert & Babs Powell by Pellier Events

Unless otherwise credited, all celebrity photographs have been provided for use in this
book and associated activity by the celebrities or their representatives.

Pasta has been eaten for centuries but it is only in the last hundred and fifty years that it has become one of the staples of every kitchen. There are hundreds of different types of pasta and many more combinations of sauces, toppings, fillings and flavours. In this book we have tried to give you a selection of delicious, easy to prepare dishes that embody the essence of good old fashioned Italian cooking with a modern British twist. Try unusual yet mouth-watering dishes like Tagliatelle with Gorgonzola and Deep-Fried Sage or old favourites like Spaghetti Amatriciana.

ASK was the first branded Italian restaurant in the UK. It has been loved by millions since it began in 1993 in a converted house in Haverstock Hill. This was the first chance for many to experience authentic Italian food and the word quickly spread. Now with over 120 restaurants across the country ASK has become the nation's favourite Italian. True to its origins, ASK continues to be popular for regular everyday occasions when reliability of food, environment and service is very important. The restaurant's success continues to be based around good quality and generous portions of Italian classics.

The celebrities in this book are amongst the leaders in their fields. These individuals from the worlds of film, music, television, comedy, literature, cooking, fashion and entertainment have all come together as part of ASK's campaign to raise funds for Great Ormond Street Hospital Children's Charity. They are participating voluntarily for which we are very grateful. Some of them have friends and family who have benefited from the support that the hospital offers while others are new supporters. It is a testament to the special affection that Great Ormond Street Hospital's work generates that we have managed to assemble such a great collection of celebrity supporters. ASK are delighted to once again be supporting Great Ormond Street Hospital Children's Charity and are honoured to be recognised as an official partner of such an inspirational institution.

It's a place where amazing things happen every day. The contributions from this book and the special dishes at ASK will make a difference to the children and their families who rely on Great Ormond Street Hospital every day.

FOREWORD
BY TESS DALY & VERNON KAY
*Patrons, Great Ormond Street Hospital
Children's Charity*

Tess and Vernon join a group of patients at the breaking ground ceremony for the new Morgan Stanley Clinical Building at Great Ormond Street Hospital where the kitchen funded by ASK will be situated.

Great Ormond Street Hospital does amazing work.

Over a period of time we have got to know about Great Ormond Street Hospital and the fantastic work that's done there. We're very proud to be patrons and hope that by lending our support we can help the thousands of patients that go through Great Ormond Street Hospital's doors each year.

We have been honoured to be involved with Great Ormond Street Hospital Children's Charity and to support their wide variety of events and campaigns. This book produced on their behalf by ASK is one of the most innovative ways of fundraising we've been involved with and by buying this book you have directly supported this incredibly worthwhile organisation full of remarkable children whose bravery touches everyone.

This book will be sold for £5 at ASK restaurants with £4 going directly to Great Ormond Street Hospital Children's Charity with the aim of building a much needed new kitchen in the hospital.

With the help of supporters like you Great Ormond Street Hospital will help keep the magic alive for thousands of children who need their help every year.

THANK YOU

Shane Richie

Award-winning and versatile, actor Shane Ritchie's career has spanned theatre, musicals, film and television.

INGREDIENTS

2 tbsp olive oil • 2 chicken breast sliced and seasoned with olive oil, salt & pepper • 2 garlic cloves finely chopped • 1 fresh green chilli chopped • 1 x 450g can chopped tomatoes • Handful chopped flat leaf parsley • Salt and pepper to season • 300g penne

PENNE POLLO ARRABBIATA

Meaning 'angry' in English, Arrabbiata is a spicy sauce for hot-blooded people. Gluttons for punishment are welcome to add even more chilli.

1 In a large frying pan warm the oil on medium heat. Add the chicken and stir-fry until sealed. Add the garlic and chilli and cook until garlic starts to brown.

2 Add the tomatoes to the pan, season well with salt and pepper, bring to boil, and then reduce heat, simmer for 8 to 10 minutes.

3 Place a large pan of water on high heat and add a pinch of salt.

4 When it's bubbling rapidly pop in the pasta, being careful to separate it with a fork to prevent sticking. Cook until al dente.

5 Drain the pasta and toss together with the sauce and half the parsley.

6 Serve at once in a warm serving dish and sprinkle with a little more chopped parsley.

PREPARATION TIME: 10 MINUTES COOKING TIME: 25 MINUTES SERVES 2

PENNE POLLO
ARRABBIATA

02

Omid
Djalali

Not content with sell-out comedy tours and appearances in movies such as 'Notting Hill', 'Spy Game' and 'The Mummy', The award-winning actor and comedian has recently performed the role of Fagin in the musical 'Oliver!' to critical acclaim.

INGREDIENTS

• 4 tbsp extra virgin olive oil • ½ onion, chopped • 600g fresh or frozen peas • Handful of fresh chopped mint
• Seasoning • 300g tripoline pasta (or any ribbon pasta such as tagliatelle / fettuccine if you prefer)

TRIPOLINE WITH MINT AND PEAS

Don't shy from frozen peas if seasonal peas aren't available. Double cream could be added at the pea purée stage – if you're feeling in a luxurious mood!

1 Heat the oil in a large pan, add the onion and cook gently for 3 minutes, without letting it brown. Add the peas and mint and 200ml boiling water. Cook over a medium heat for about 15 minutes or until the peas are tender (frozen peas should only take about 8 minutes).

2 When the peas are tender, remove from the heat, take out about half the peas and purée them in a food processor. Put the puréed peas back into the pan with the whole peas.

3 Place a large pan of water on high heat and add a pinch of salt.

4 When it's bubbling rapidly pop in the pasta, and separate with a fork to prevent sticking. Cook until al dente (around 8 minutes).

5 Drain the pasta and return to the pan, add the peas and mix well. Serve with peas and love!

PREPARATION TIME: 10 MINUTES COOKING TIME: 10 MINUTES SERVES: 4

TRIPOLINE WITH MINT AND PEAS

Michael Palin CBE

Traveller, explorer, comedian, writer, television presenter, actor and of course Python, Michael Palin has helped deliver us some of our most memorable moments – from 'Pole to Pole' and 'The Lumberjack Song' to 'The Dead Parrot' .

03

INGREDIENTS

85g unsalted butter • 4 tbsp virgin olive oil • 2 large skinless chicken breasts cut into strips • Handful each chopped parsley, chives and mint • 200g baby carrots, halved • 400g peas freshly podded • 200g green beans, trimmed • 200g baby courgettes, halved • Finely-grated zest and juice of 1 lemon • A handful of basil leaves • Seasoning • 400g pappardelle or tagliatelle

PAPPARDELLE WITH VEGETABLES & CHICKEN

This fresh dish is like a stroll through a country garden. For a more marine alternative, swap the chicken with prawns or skip it altogether to make a great veggie option.

1 Gently melt the butter with 1 tablespoon of oil in a pan. Add the chicken and stir-fry for 4-5 minutes or until cooked thoroughly. Add the parsley, chives and mint, mix and set to one side.

2 Place two large pans of water on high heat and add a pinch of salt.

3 When they are bubbling rapidly pop the pasta into one, being careful to separate it with a fork to stop sticking. Cook until al dente (around 8 minutes).

4 Add the carrots to the other pan and cook for 2 minutes. Add the peas, green beans and courgettes and continue to cook for 3 minutes. Drain both the pasta and the vegetables.

5 Return the pasta and vegetables to the hot pan and toss with the rest of the olive oil, the herb butter and the lemon zest and juice. Sprinkle generously with basil, salt and black pepper and eat, ideally, surrounded by green, rolling hills.

PREPARATION TIME: 10 MINUTES COOKING TIME: 20 MINUTES SERVES: 4

David Coulthard

After moving into Formula One in 1995 DC went on to win thirteen grand prix, including two at Monaco. He holds the British record for podium finishes with 62 and is the highest-scoring British driver ever with 535 points.

04

INGREDIENTS

16 tbsp extra virgin olive oil • 2 cloves garlic, crushes • Large pinch chilli flakes • 4 tbsp freshly chopped flat leaf parsley • 450g spaghetti

SPAGHETTI WITH OLIVE OIL & GARLIC

For a quick and delicious dish, this is pasta in its purest form. Beware though; the quality of this dish depends on your olive oil, so use the best that you can lay your hands on!

1 Place a large pan of water on high heat and add a pinch of salt.

2 When it's bubbling rapidly pop in the pasta, being careful to separate with a fork to prevent sticking. Cook until al dente (around 8 minutes).

3 Heat the oil in a frying pan. Add the garlic and chilli flakes and heat for about 20 seconds. Don't let the garlic colour. Add the parsley.

4 Spoon all the contents of the frying pan over the drained spaghetti and toss.

PREPARATION TIME: 5 MINUTES COOKING TIME: 10 MINUTES SERVES: 4

SPAGHETTI WITH OLIVE OIL & GARLIC

05

Simon Schama CBE

One of Britain's most recognizable historians and art historians, Simon is perhaps best known for his groundbreaking 'A History of Britain' series for the BBC.

INGREDIENTS

2 tbsp olive oil, chopped • 1 large red onion, diced • 2 sticks celery, diced • 450g pack ground Veal • 1 tbsp plain flour • 150ml red wine • 4 bay leaves • 500ml hot vegetable stock • Seasoning • 350g spirali pasta

SPIRALI VEAL RAGU

This fabulous rustic dish from the Italian countryside is earthy, homely and perfect to serve on a winter's evening.

1 Heat 1 tbsp oil in a large pan over a medium heat. Cook the onion and celery, stirring occasionally, for 5 minutes or until softened. Remove from pan and set aside.

2 Return pan to the heat and when hot again add the veal. Cook for about 8 minutes stirring occasionally to brown evenly and break up all the clumps of meat.

3 Return the onion and celery to the pan and stir in the flour. Add the wine, bay leaves and stock. Bring to the boil then reduce the heat and leave to simmer for about 1 hour, uncovered — check every now and again in case you need to add more water.

4 Place a large pan of water on high heat and add a pinch of salt.

5 When it's bubbling rapidly pop in the pasta, being careful to separate it with a fork to prevent sticking. Cook until al dente (around 8 minutes).

6 Drain the pasta and return to the pan. Add the veal ragu and serve alongside a full-bodied glass of Italian red.

**PREPARATION TIME: 5 MINUTES COOKING TIME: 1 HOUR 35 MINUTES
SERVES: 4**

Zoë
Wanamaker
CBE

"I'm so happy to support such a
wonderful cause — and in such
a mouth watering-way."

INGREDIENTS

12 tbsp olive oil • 1 large carrot, peeled and finely diced • 1 celery stick, finely diced • 1 onion, finely diced
• 2 garlic cloves, crushed • 750g minced beef steak • 1 tbsp tomato purée • 50g butter • 50g plain flour
• 568ml full-fat milk • 100g Parmesan, grated • 9 lasagne sheets

BEEF LASAGNE

The most famous of all Italian classic dishes — always a showstopper!

1   Heat the oil in a large saucepan. Add the carrot, celery,
onion and garlic and cook over a medium heat for 5
minutes or until the onion is beautifully translucent. Add
the mince and cook for 5 minutes, stirring and break up all
the clumps of meat. Cook until the mince is evenly brown.

2   Stir in the tomato purée and cook for 1 minute. Add enough
cold water to cover the meat and bring to a simmer. Cover
and cook for 2 hours. Check every now again in case you
may need at top up with water. Uncover for the final 30
minutes and simmer until you have a rich Bolognese sauce.

3   Preheat the oven to 200°C/fan 180°C/400°F/Gas mark 6.

4   When the mince is nearly ready, make the béchamel sauce.
Melt the butter in a pan over a medium heat. Stir in the
flour and cook for 1 minute. Remove from the heat and
gradually whisk in the milk. Return to the heat and bring to
the boil, stirring constantly. Reduce the heat slightly and
simmer for 5 minutes, stirring until thickened. Stir in 2
tablespoons Parmesan, season and set aside.

5   Now layer the lasagne. Spread a little of the Bolognese
sauce in the base of a deep, 2.25-litre ovenproof dish. Add
3 lasagne sheets in 1 layer, cutting them if need be. Add a
third of the béchamel sauce and a sprinkling of Parmesan,
and then top with half the meat. Make another layer of 3
lasagne sheets, then spread with a third of the béchamel
and a sprinkling of Parmesan. Spoon over the remaining
Bolognese sauce. Add a final layer of 3 lasagne sheets
and spread the rest of the béchamel on top. Sprinkle with
the remaining Parmesan. Cover with foil and bake for 40
minutes, then uncover and bake for 8-10 minutes until
deep golden. Serve to a round of applause and several
offers of marriage.

PREPARATION TIME: 10 MINUTES   COOKING TIME: 2 HOURS 20 MINUTES   SERVES: 4

Sorry: In our excitement to get all of these wonderful recipes printed and start raising funds for Great Ormond Street Hospital Children's Charity, the Peppered Pork & Red Pepper Pasta recipe has been printed incorrectly. This insert shows the correct method to make this flavoursome dish.

07

Angela
Rippon OBE

Initially known as a television journalist and newsreader, Angela is one of the country's most successful television presenters having hosted shows as diverse as 'Come Dancing', 'Top Gear' and 'What's My Line?'

INGREDIENTS

300g pack pork strips • 2 tbsp olive oil • 2 red peppers, deseeded and cut into large cubes • 2 red onions, sliced • 1 tbsp balsamic vinegar • 1 tbsp clear honey • Seasoning • Handful fresh sage • 300g tagliatelle

PEPPERED PORK & RED PEPPER PASTA

Even though Marco Polo didn't in fact bring pasta back from China to Italy, we're sure he would have been proud of this fabulous east meets west sweet-and-sour pasta dish.

1 Season the pork with pepper and set aside.

2 Place a large pan of water on high heat and add a pinch of salt.

3 When it's bubbling rapidly pop in the pasta, being careful to separate it with a fork to prevent sticking. Cook until al dente (around 8 minutes).

4 Heat half the oil in a large frying pan. Add the peppers and onions and stir over a medium heat, until just soft and lightly golden. Remove from the pan and set aside.

5 Heat the remaining oil in the pan over a high heat. Add the pork and stir fry for 3-4 minutes or until thoroughly cooked and the juices run clear.

6 Add the peppers and onions. Drizzle with the balsamic vinegar and honey and season. Add to the drained pasta and toss with the sage.

PREPARATION TIME: 15 MINUTES COOKING TIME: 20 MINUTES SERVES: 4

PEPPERED PORK &
RED PEPPER PASTA

Angela Rippon OBE

Initially known as a television journalist and newsreader, Angela is one of the country's most successful television presenters having hosted shows as diverse as 'Come Dancing', 'Top Gear' and 'What's My Line?'

INGREDIENTS

300g pack pork strips • 2 tbsp olive oil • 2 red peppers, deseeded and cut into large cubes • 2 red onions, sliced • 1 tbsp balsamic vinegar • 1 tbsp clear honey • Seasoning • Handful fresh sage • 300g tagliatelle

PEPPERED PORK & RED PEPPER PASTA

Even though Marco Polo didn't in fact bring pasta back from China to Italy, we're sure he would have been proud of this fabulous east meets west sweet-and-sour pasta dish.

1   For the filling, heat a large pan on a medium heat and add the butter. Once melted, add the crushed garlic and gently fry for a minute. Add the spinach and toss in the garlicky butter. Add a sprinkling of nutmeg and season. Stir until the spinach has wilted. Drain and dry thoroughly with kitchen paper. Allow to cool before roughly chopping, then set aside.

2   In a large bowl, mix the ricotta, Parmesan, pine nuts and egg yolk together. Mix in the spinach and lightly season. Cool in the fridge until ready to use.

3   Preheat the oven to 180°C/ 160°C, 350°F/ gas mark 4.

4   Next make the tomato sauce. Heat the olive oil in a pan to a medium heat, add the onion and gently cook without colouring; this will take a minimum of 5 minutes. Add the garlic and repeat the process, cooking slowly.

5   Add the salt, pepper, dried chilli and basil, followed by the tomatoes. Bring this to a simmer and cook gently for 10 minutes or until the sauce is deliciously thick.

6   Spoon the ricotta filling into the cannelloni tubes – this can be done using a spoon or a piping bag.

7   Spread a layer of tomato sauce in the base of two ovenproof dishes and lay your cannelloni in it. Try to keep the pasta tubes tight against each other. Cover with the remaining sauce and grate fresh Parmesan over the whole dish.

8   Place in the oven for 20 to 25 minutes, or until golden brown. Serve with a crisp salad.

PREPARATION TIME: 15 MINUTES COOKING TIME: 20 MINUTES SERVES: 4

PEPPERED PORK & RED PEPPER PASTA

08

Dame Judi Dench

Considered by many to be one of the greatest British actresses of the post-war period, her theatre and film work have won her numerous accolades including an incredible 10 BAFTA's and 6 Academy Award nominations.

INGREDIENTS

2 tbsps olive oil • 80g pancetta • 300g mussels, scrubbed and debearded • 2 cloves garlic chopped • 250ml single cream • 50ml cooking white wine • Handful fresh chopped flat leaf parsley • Salt and pepper • 300g linguine

LINGUINE DEL PORTO

Don't be intimidated by fresh mussels – all you have to do is wash them and discard any damaged ones first.

1 Heat oil in a pan, add the pancetta and cook until crispy and brown. Add in the mussels and cook until all the mussels have all opened up (about 4-5 minutes). Discard any that remain closed.

2 Add the garlic and cook on low heat so that the garlic is not burnt.

3 Pour in the single cream and cooking wine and add the flat leaf parsley. Season and heat gently on low heat until the cream starts to thicken.

4 Place a large pan of water on high heat and add a pinch of salt.

5 When it's bubbling rapidly pop in the pasta, being careful to separate it with a fork to prevent sticking. Cook until al dente (around 8 minutes).

6 Drain the pasta and toss with the sauce, serve immediately in a warm serving dish and garnish with a pinch of flat leaf parsley. Don't forget to provide an extra dish for all the shells.

PREPARATION TIME: 5 MINUTES COOKING TIME: 15 MINUTES SERVES 2

Debbie Chazen

Actress whose starring TV roles include 'We are Klang', 'The Smoking Room' and 'Titty Bang Bang'. This acclaimed theatre performer recently starred in 'Calendar Girls' in the West End in a part in which she is most definitely on show!

INGREDIENTS

6 tbsp extra virgin olive oil • 1 medium onion, finely chopped • 2 fat garlic cloves, chopped • 150g pancetta or streaky bacon, finely chopped • 225g lean minced beef • 225g minced pork • 100g chicken livers, trimmed, washed and dried • 1x 400g tin chopped tomatoes • 1x 200g tube double concentrate tomato purée • 350ml red wine • Seasoning • Parmesan, to serve • 300g spaghetti

SPAGHETTI BOLOGNESE

Try this version for a truly luxurious Bolognese experience.

1   Preheat the oven to 140°C/fan 120°C/275°F/Gas mark 1.

2   Find your largest frying pan and heat 3 tbsp olive oil. Add the onion and garlic and cook slowly over a low heat for 10 minutes – this should give you beautifully caramelized but not burnt onions. Add the pancetta and cook for a further 5 minutes. Transfer this mixture to a large casserole.

3   Add another tablespoon of oil to the pan, turn the heat to high and add the beef mince. Cook until brown, moving it consistently so all the clumps are broken up. Add to the casserole dish. Heat another tablespoon of the oil and repeat with the minced pork. When ready, add to the casserole.

4   Heat the remaining tablespoon of oil and brown the pieces of chicken liver. Add these to the casserole.

5   Place the casserole over the direct heat, and stir in the tomatoes, purée, and red wine and season well. Bring the whole lot to a simmer, then place in the oven and cook for about 3 hours. You could eat it after 2 hours, but the longer you cook it the more intense the flavours will be.

6   When nearly done, place a large pan of water on high heat and add a pinch of salt.

7   When it's bubbling rapidly pop in the pasta, being careful to separate it with a fork to prevent sticking. Cook until al dente (around 8 minutes).

8   Drain the spaghetti, return to the pan and mix thoroughly with the Bolognese. Serve with shavings of Parmesan. Enjoy!

PREPARATION TIME: 25 MINUTES   COOKING TIME: 3 HOURS   SERVES: 4

10

Ed Baines

Ed launched his career as head chef at Daphne's before opening his flagship restaurant Randall & Aubin. Ed is a regular chef on shows like '…Cooks!', 'Saturday Kitchen' and 'This Morning' and is a judge on 'Britain's Best Dish'.

INGREDIENTS

200g asparagus • Knob of butter • 3 tbsp extra virgin olive oil • 300g lobster meat, cubed • Splash of white wine • 300ml double cream • Handful basil, chopped • Seasoning • 300g linguine

ASPARAGUS & LOBSTER PASTA

There is true class in this elegant combination. However if you have the class and the elegance, but not the full budget, swap tiger prawns or langoustines in for the lobster.

1 Place a large pan of water on high heat and add a pinch of salt.

2 When it's bubbling rapidly pop in the pasta, being careful to separate it with a fork to prevent sticking. Cook until al dente (around 8 minutes).

3 Blanch the asparagus in boiling water for 4 minutes. Drain and refresh in cold water. Chop into 4 cm pieces.

4 Heat the butter and oil in a frying pan, add the lobster meat and cook for 3 minutes. Add the asparagus and a splash of wine.

5 Pour in the cream and stir in the basil. Leave to simmer until the cream has thickened slightly.

6 Drain the pasta and add the sauce. Toss gently and season.

PREPARATION TIME: 10 MINUTES COOKING TIME: 20 MINUTES SERVES: 2

01 Cooked al dente literally means "to the tooth," which is how to test pasta to see if it is properly cooked. The pasta should be a bit firm, offering some resistance to the tooth but still tender. Different pastas become al dente at different speeds.

03 **02** The word "pasta" comes from the Italian for paste. The paste in question is a combination of flour and water.

"It will be maccheroni, I swear to you, that will unite Italy."
GIUSEPPE GARIBALDI, ON LIBERATING NAPLES IN 1860

04 Chili peppers have been a part of the human diet in the Americas since at least 7500 BC and are one of the first cultivated crops in the Americas that are self-pollinating.

05 One of the earliest documents referring to pasta is a book of recipes written shortly after the birth of Christ by a chef named Apicius, who describes "lagane" as similar to present day lasagna.

06 Homer (the epic poet not the Simpson) called olive oil "liquid gold." Despite its great value ancient Greek athletes ritually rubbed it all over their bodies.

Dan Antopolski

Inventive and intelligent, Dan has garnered himself three Perrier Award nominations and has won many awards including the BBC New Comedy Award & Best Joke at the Edinburgh Festival.

"I tried to trace the origins of spaghetti bolognese, but I gave up as I couldn't find the source."

ALL ABOUT PASTA

07 The Spanish explorer Cortez brought tomatoes back to Europe from Mexico in 1519. It would take nearly three centuries before pasta with tomato sauce became a staple in Italian kitchens.

08 Garlic has been used as both food and medicine for thousands of years. Its properties are mentioned by many notable figures including Hippocrates, Galen and Pliny as well as being recorded in both the Bible and the Talmud.

09 On April Fool's Day 1957 the BBC's Panorama programme broadcast a report on the bumper Swiss spaghetti harvest occurring beside Lake Lugano. Footage showing 'spaghetti trees' was watched by over 8 million people and led to hundreds of people trying to grow their own spaghetti trees before it was revealed as a hoax.

10 "A piece of spaghetti or a military unit can only be led from the front end."
GEORGE S. PATTON

11 Pine nuts have been eaten in Europe and Asia since the Paleolithic period.

12 The earliest reference to pasta was found in an Etruscan tomb dating to about 400 BC where a series of engravings of tools used for making and cooking pasta was found in a cave about 30 miles north of modern day Rome.

Mick Hucknall

"I first had this dish in 1986, close to Imperia on the Italian riviera, precisely as it is in this recipe. It's remained a firm favourite of mine ever since."

INGREDIENTS

6 tbsp extra-virgin olive oil • 2 cloves of garlic, chopped • Good pinch of dried chilli flakes • Small bunch of fresh parsley, finely chopped • 1kg small clams, scrubbed and de-gritted • 100ml dry white wine • Salt and pepper • 450g linguine

LINGUINE VONGOLE

This clam dish is a happy mainstay on any Italian menu.

1 Place a large pan of water on high heat and add a pinch of salt.

2 When it's bubbling rapidly pop in the pasta, being careful to separate it with a fork to prevent sticking. Cook until al dente (around 8 minutes).

3 In another pan, heat half the olive oil and cook the garlic, chilli and half the parsley for a couple of minutes; but don't let the garlic burn. Add the clams and wine, turn up the heat, then cover. Cook for 4-5 minutes, or until the clams have opened. Discard any clams that have not opened.

4 Toss the clams and the juices with the drained linguine and remaining parsley. Season, and add the remaining olive oil. Toss and serve with a chilled glass of white wine.

PREPARATION TIME: 10 MINUTES COOKING TIME: 20 MINUTES SERVES: 4

12

One of the world's greatest ever mountaineers, his career has included 19 expeditions to the Himalayas including four to Mount Everest. He led the first successful ascent of the south face of Annapurna.

INGREDIENTS

3 cloves garlic, crushed • 255g yellow cherry tomatoes, halved • 255g red cherry tomatoes, halved • Handful black olives, pitted • Handful fresh chives, snipped • Handful fresh basil • ½ cucumber, diced • 4 spring onions, sliced • 2 cooked chicken breasts, shredded • 4 tbsp white wine vinegar, or to taste • 7 tbsp extra virgin olive oil • Sea salt and freshly ground black pepper • 300g casarecce pasta (or small shell pasta)

SUMMER PASTA SALAD

A fresh and light picnic addition or BBQ accompaniment. Chill for an hour to intensify the flavours and refresh the temperature.

1 Place a large pan of water on high heat and add a pinch of salt.

2 When it's bubbling rapidly pop in the pasta and garlic, careful to separate it with a fork to prevent sticking. Cook until al dente (around 8 minutes).

3 Drain and rinse under cold water to cool. Save the garlic for later. Put the pasta into a bowl. Add the tomatoes, olives, chives, basil, cucumber and spring onions and shredded chicken.

4 Squash the garlic cloves out of their skins and place in a mini processor. Add the vinegar and olive oil and seasoning. Whiz until amalgamated. Drizzle this over the salad, and toss.

5 Serve at room temperature.

PREPARATION TIME: 10 MINUTES COOKING TIME: 8 MINUTES SERVES: 4

Christopher Biggins

The much loved actor of stage and screen and Britain's favourite pantomime 'Dame' has only missed one season in over 30 years when he was taking part in 'I'm a Celebrity… Get Me Out of Here!' where he was voted the winner.

13

INGREDIENTS

5 tbsp olive oil • 4 chicken breasts • 1 onion, finely chopped • 2 garlic cloves, crushed • 2 x 400g tins cherry tomatoes • 2 tbsp red wine vinegar • Pinch sugar • 4 tbsp mascarpone • Handful basil, roughly ripped • 350g farfalle pasta

FARFALLE ALLA CACCIATORE

This 'Hunter's pasta' (cacciatore) is traditionally a concoction of what a hunter might find in his pouch come dinner time. A spot of mascarpone is the only luxury here, and you'll find the cherry tomatoes add a sweetening balance to the tangy chicken.

1 Heat the oven to 190°C/fan 170°C/375°F/Gas mark 5.

2 Heat a little oil in a pan and fry the chicken on both sides until golden. Transfer to a baking tray and cook for 25-30 minutes or until the chicken is cooked through.

3 Heat 3 tbsp oil in a large frying pan. Add the onion and garlic and cook until softened but not coloured. Add the tomatoes, red wine vinegar and a pinch of sugar. Season, and then simmer for 10-15 minutes or until thick and glossy. When ready take off the heat and stir in the mascarpone and half the basil.

4 Place a large pan of water on high heat and add a pinch of salt.

5 When it's bubbling rapidly pop in the pasta, being careful to separate it with a fork to prevent sticking. Cook until al dente (around 8 minutes).

6 Drain the pasta and toss with the tomato sauce. Mix in the chicken or serve the dish topped with the slices for a gourmet presentation.

PREPARATION TIME: 5 MINUTES COOKING TIME: 45 MINUTES SERVES: 4

Claudia Winkleman

A dynamic television presenter, radio personality and journalist, Claudia has hosted shows ranging from 'Hell's Kitchen', 'Strictly Come Dancing' and 'Comic Relief Does Fame Academy'.

INGREDIENTS

1 tbsp olive oil • ¼ red onion, sliced • ½ tsp dried chilli flakes • 1 chorizo sausages, cubed • 55g tomato purée • 55g sun-blushed tomatoes, chopped • 200ml red wine • Seasoning • Basil leaves to garnish • 300g pennoni pasta

PENNONI WITH SPICY CHORIZO

Italian romance meets Iberian passion with fiery results in this succulent dish.

1 Heat the oil in a frying pan over a medium to high heat. Add the onion and chilli and cook for about 2 minutes.

2 Add the chorizo and cook for 5 minutes, or until golden brown all over and all the juices have oozed out. Add the tomato purée, sun blushed tomatoes and red wine. Simmer for 15 minutes. Season.

3 Place a large pan of water on high heat and add a pinch of salt.

4 When it's bubbling rapidly pop in the pasta, being careful to separate it with a fork to prevent sticking. Cook until al dente (around 10 minutes).

5 Drain the pasta and add to the sauce. Leave to stand for a few minutes so the pasta absorbs all the succulent chorizo juices.
Serve with a delicate garnish of fresh basil and a flamenco flourish!

PREPARATION TIME: 5 MINUTES COOKING TIME: 25 MINUTES SERVES: 4

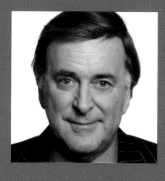

15

Sir Terry Wogan

A 'national treasure' with a career in broadcasting that has spanned over 40 years, Terry's voice has become the most listened to and loved on the radio.

INGREDIENTS

2 tbsps olive oil • 2 garlic cloves finely chopped • 2 tbsps capers • 450g of canned chopped tomatoes • 150g canned tuna fish, drained • 50ml cooking white wine • 8 anchovies fillets in oil, drained • 25g black pitted Kalamata olives • 1 tsp fresh chopped dill • Salt and pepper, to season • ½ lemon wedge • 300g fusilli

FUSILLI PUTTANESCA

Meaning 'lady of the night', this could be described as the sauciest of sauces. It's spicy, tangy and dripping with the taste of the Mediterranean.

1. Heat oil in a pan, add the garlic and capers and heat until the caper split. Add garlic and lightly brown.

2. Add tomatoes and tuna, season with salt and pepper and simmer on low heat for 8 to 10 minutes.

3. Add the wine, anchovies and olives and cook for a further 5 minutes. Stir the dill through the sauce.

4. Place a large pan of water on high heat and add a pinch of salt.

5. When it's bubbling rapidly pop in the pasta, being careful to separate it with a fork to prevent sticking. Cook until al dente.

6. Toss the sauce with the drained pasta and serve immediately in a warm serving dish. Squeeze the lemon over the top or serve with a lemon wedge for an extra tarty twist!

PREPARATION TIME: 5 MINUTES COOKING TIME: 15 MINUTES SERVES 2

FUSILLI PUTTANESCA

16

Denise Welch

As an actress she has appeared in many of our most popular TV shows including 'Coronation Street', 'Soldier Soldier' and 'Spender'. She has also well known as a presenter and is a regular panellist on daytime chat show 'Loose Women'.

INGREDIENTS

600g butternut squash, peeled and cut into 2cm cubes • 1 red onion, cut into wedges • 4 tbsp extra virgin olive oil • 50g pine nuts, toasted • Handful sage leaves, ripped • 100g soft goat's cheese, crumbled • 450g spirali pasta

SPIRALI WITH BUTTERNUT SQUASH

Butternut squash is a good rustic wintry ingredient, and goes stunningly well partnered with crumbly goat's cheese in this seasonal mixture.

1 Preheat the oven to 200°C/fan 180°C/400°F/Gas mark 6.

2 Toss the butternut squash and onion in the oil. Spoon onto a baking tin and roast for 25 minutes until soft and lightly charred. Add the pine nuts and sage and cook for a further 10 minutes.

3 Place a large pan of water on high heat and add a pinch of salt.

4 When it's bubbling rapidly pop in the pasta, being careful to separate it with a fork to prevent sticking. Cook until al dente (around 8 minutes).

5 Drain the pasta, return to the pan and add the remaining olive oil, goat's cheese and all the contents of the baking tin. Toss and season well.

PREPARATION TIME: 10 MINUTES COOKING TIME: 45 MINUTES SERVES: 4

SPIRALI WITH BUTTERNUT SQUASH

Gregg Wallace

Writer, television presenter and fruit & veg supremo, Gregg presents 'Masterchef' where he is known as an "ingredients expert". Gregg also judges 'Masterchef: The professionals' alongside double Michelin star holder Michel Roux Jr.

INGREDIENTS

4 small courgettes, sliced • 20 cherry tomatoes, halved • 4 tbsp extra virgin olive oil • 2 cloves garlic, crushed • Sea salt and pepper • 3 skinless chicken breast, cubed • 1 tbsp fresh thyme leaves • 300g conchiglie

CONCHIGLIE WITH ROASTED VEGETABLES

For a Sunday roast in pasta form, try this fine winter's dish, replete with roast chicken and tasty vegetables. Ramp it up with extra roast veggies as you see fit, such as red peppers and red onion.

1 Heat the oven to 200°C/fan 180°/400°F/Gas mark 6.

2 Toss the courgettes and tomatoes in half the olive oil, garlic, sea salt and pepper. Arrange on a baking tray lined with greaseproof paper and bake for 20 minutes until the courgettes start to brown and the tomatoes are squishy.

3 On a separate baking tray, toss the chicken with the rest of the olive oil and thyme. Bake for 20 minutes or until thoroughly cooked.

4 Place a large pan of water on high heat and add a pinch of salt.

5 When it's bubbling rapidly pop in the pasta, being careful to separate it with a fork to prevent sticking. Cook until al dente (around 8 minutes).

6 Drain the pasta and return to the pan. Add the roast vegetables and chicken and any juices from the tray, toss well and prepare to be warmed and nourished.

PREPARATION TIME: 10 MINUTES COOKING TIME: 25 MINUTES SERVES: 4

Dylan Jones

Writer and journalist Dylan Jones has been the editor of a diverse range of publications including 'Arena', 'i-D', 'The Face', 'The Observer Magazine' and 'The Sunday Times'. He is currently the editor of 'GQ UK'.

18

INGREDIENTS

4 tbsp virgin olive oil • 1 clove garlic, finely sliced • 1 red chilli, deseeded and finely chopped • About 300g mixed seafood e.g. prawns, mussels, scallops, squid • Finely-grated zest and juice of 1 lemon, plus lemon wedges to serve • Handful chopped fresh mint leaves • Handful chopped fresh flat-leaf parsley • Seasoning • 200g spaghetti (or linguine if you like)

SEAFOOD SPAGHETTI

For those who love a bit of ocean spray, this dish can be fitted to all budgets and palates. It works great with a supermarket bag of mixed seafood or titbits from your fishmonger if you want to push the boat out.

1   Place a large pan of water on high heat and add a pinch of salt.

2   When it's bubbling rapidly pop in the pasta, being careful to separate it with a fork to prevent sticking. Cook until al dente (around 8 minutes)

3   In a large frying pan warm the oil on medium heat. Add the garlic and chilli and cook for 30 seconds, don't let them colour.

4   Toss your seafood in the oil and cook for 5 minutes or until piping hot. Mix it in with the drained pasta along with the lemon juice, lemon zest and the fresh herbs.

5   Finally season, toss well, and serve with a lemon wedge and a smile.

PREPARATION TIME: 5 MINUTES   COOKING TIME: 10 MINUTES   SERVES: 2

19

Dame
Vivienne
Westwood

The iconic fashion designer whose style and influence continues to be felt globally and has perfectly combined cutting edge and often seemingly outrageous ideas with traditional fabrics and design elements.

INGREDIENTS

12 sage leaves • 200g Gorgonzola • 150ml milk • 50g butter • 100ml double cream • Parmesan, to serve • 300g tagliatelle

TAGLIATELLE WITH GORGONZOLA & DEEP-FRIED SAGE

This excellent strong-smelling cheese is a favourite in northern Italy. For those who can't quite deal with it, another alternative is left-over Stilton or Dolcelatte.

1 Heat the oil in a small saucepan. Add the sage leaves and fry until crispy. Drain on kitchen paper until ready to use.

2 Place a large pan of water on high heat and add a pinch of salt.

3 When it's bubbling rapidly pop in the pasta, being careful to separate it with a fork to prevent sticking. Cook until al dente (around 8 minutes).

4 Place half the Gorgonzola, milk and butter in a small saucepan. Heat and stir gently until just melted. Add the cream and cook until the cream has thickened and reduced slightly.

5 Drain the pasta and return to the pan. Pour in the Gorgonzola cream. Break the remaining Gorgonzola into cubes and add to the pan.

6 Serve with gratings of Parmesan and the deep fried sage. A truly luxurious dairy experience.

PREPARATION TIME: 10 MINUTES COOKING TIME: 15 MINUTES SERVES: 4

TAGLIATELLE WITH GORGONZOLA
& DEEP-FRIED SAGE

Eoin Colfer

20

The award-winning and best selling author is best known for creating the 'Artemis Fowl' series of books. He was recently commissioned to write the sixth installment in 'The Hitchhiker's Guide To The Galaxy' series.

INGREDIENTS

150ml extra virgin olive oil • 3 cloves garlic, finely chopped • 100g pancetta cubes • Pinch chilli flakes, optional • Pinch salt • Pinch sugar • 1 x 400g can tomatoes with garlic • 125g mozzarella • 300g penne

PENNE WITH BACON & TOMATO

Some things in life were made to go together, and tomato, bacon and cheese is one of those sacred combinations.

1 In a heavy-based saucepan heat the oil. Add the garlic, pancetta, chilli flakes, and a pinch of salt and sugar. Cook for about 3 minutes, until soft but not coloured.

2 Add the tomatoes to the pan and simmer slowly for 15 minutes.

3 Place a large pan of water on high heat and add a pinch of salt.

4 When it's bubbling rapidly pop in the pasta and garlic, careful to separate it with a fork to prevent sticking. Cook until al dente (around 8 minutes).

5 Drain the pasta and add to the sauce. Rip the mozzarella into the pan and mix thoroughly. Serve immediately just as the mozzarella begins to melt, and savour the succulent flavours.

PREPARATION TIME: 5 MINUTES   COOKING TIME: 15 MINUTES   SERVES: 4

13 The Roman naturalist and philosopher Pliny the Elder recommended that a wreath of mint was a good thing for students to wear since it would "exhilarate their minds".

14 The first laws regarding the fishing of the Atlantic salmon were started over 700 years ago by Edward I of England. Alexander II of Scotland followed this up in 1318 by outlawing salmon traps in rivers. Their collective noun is a bind of salmon.

15 Meaning 'little tongues' in Italian, linguine is the typical pasta used with seafood.

16 "He who looks at magnitude / Is often mistaken. A grain of pepper conquers / Lasagna with its strength."
IACOPONE DA TODI (ITALIAN POET, DIED 1306)

17 In 1740, the city of Venice issued Paolo Adami a licence to open the first pasta factory. The pasta was made using an iron press powered by several young men.

18 Around the year 1000, the first documented recipe for pasta appeared in the book 'De arte Coquinaria per vermicelli e maccaroni siciliani' (The Art of Cooking Sicilian Macaroni and Vermicelli), written by the chef Martino Corno.

ALL ABOUT PASTA

19 A variation of lasagne appears in the 14th century cookbook, 'The Forme of Cury', which was used by the Master Cooks of King Richard II.

20 Contrary to popular belief Roman soldiers were not paid in salt. The word salad literally means "salted", and comes from the Roman practice of salting leaf vegetables.

21 "Life is a combination of magic and pasta."
FEDERICO FELLINI

22 It was not until 1839 that the first pasta recipe with tomatoes was documented.

23 The first American pasta factory was opened in Brooklyn, New York, in 1848, by a Frenchman named Antoine Zerega who managed the entire operation with a horse in his basement to power the machinery. He dried his spaghetti on his roof.

24 Asparagus is 'more than just a pretty face'. Asparagus is low in calories, contains no cholesterol and is healthy as it is very low in sodium. It is a good source of folic acid, potassium, and dietary fibre.

25 "Over 120 years of pasta perfection".

Since its humble beginnings in 1887, De Cecco has come to be something of a byword for exceptional pasta, which is why it is used in all ASK restaurants.

DE CECCO
dal 1887

21

Gyles
Brandreth

Broadcaster and prolific author,
Gyles is very much in demand as an
after-dinner speaker. (He also held
the world record for the longest
continuous after-dinner speech which
ran to twelve and a half hours!)

INGREDIENTS

For the filling: 15g unsalted butter • 2 cloves garlic, crushed • 125g baby spinach • Nutmeg, grated • Seasoning • 250g ricotta cheese • 80g Parmesan, grated • 50g pine nuts • 1 egg yolk • 6 cannelloni tubes

For the tomato sauce: 4 tbsp good olive oil • ½ onion, finely diced • 2 cloves garlic, shaved • 1 pinch dried chilli • 1 stem basil, chopped • 600g tinned tomatoes with herbs • Seasoning

SPINACH & RICOTTA CANNELLONI

A bit of extra prep makes for a seriously impressive dish.

1 For the filling, heat a large pan on a medium heat and add the butter. Once melted, add the crushed garlic and gently fry for a minute. Add the spinach and toss in the garlicky butter. Add a sprinkling of nutmeg and season. Stir until the spinach has wilted. Drain and dry thoroughly with kitchen paper. Allow to cool before roughly chopping, then set aside.

2 In a large bowl, mix the ricotta, Parmesan, pine nuts and egg yolk together. Mix in the spinach and lightly season. Cool in the fridge until ready to use.

3 Preheat the oven to 180°C/fan 160°C/350°F/Gas mark 4.

4 Next make the tomato sauce. Heat the olive oil in a pan to a medium heat, add the onion and gently cook without colouring; this will take a minimum of five minutes. Add the garlic and repeat the process, cooking slowly.

5 Add the salt, pepper, dried chilli and basil, followed by the tomatoes. Bring this to a simmer and cook gently for 10 minutes or until the sauce is deliciously thick.

6 Spoon the ricotta filling into the cannelloni tubes – this can be done using a spoon or a piping bag.

7 Spread a layer of tomato sauce in the base of two ovenproof dishes and lay your cannelloni in it. Try to keep the pasta tubes tight against each other. Cover with the remaining sauce and grate fresh Parmesan over the whole dish.

8 Place in the oven for 20 to 25 minutes, or until golden brown. Serve with a crisp salad.

SPINACH & RICOTTA CANNELLONI

PREPARATION TIME: 15 MINUTES COOKING TIME: 25 MINUTES SERVES: 2

22

Davina
McCall

"Great Ormond Street Hospital is a place where miracles happen every day. Where extraordinary courage, strength and love is the norm. I am hugely proud that we have such an amazing world class hospital in the UK."

INGREDIENTS

2 tbsp olive oil • 120g pancetta • 1 large onion, thinly sliced • 2 garlic cloves, finely chopped • 1 fresh green chilli, chopped • 450g of canned chopped tomatoes • Salt and pepper, to season • Handful fresh chopped flat leaf parsley to garnish • 300g spaghetti

SPAGHETTI AMATRICIANA

Hailing from Amatrice, buried in the heart of Italy to the east of Rome, this nourishing sauce was traditionally prepared with cured pork jowl. These days you'll probably have less trouble finding pancetta.

1 Heat oil in a pan, add the pancetta and onions and cook until the pancetta is crispy and brown and the onion starts to brown. Add garlic and chilli, cook until garlic starts to brown.

2 Add tomatoes and season with salt and pepper. Bring the sauce to boil then reduce the heat and simmer for 8 to 10 minutes.

3 Place a large pan of water on high heat and add a pinch of salt.

4 When it's bubbling rapidly pop in the pasta, being careful to separate it with a fork to prevent sticking. Cook until al dente.

5 When the pasta is cooked, drain and toss with the sauce, serve immediately in a warm serving dish and sprinkle lovingly with chopped parsley.

PREPARATION TIME: 5 MINUTES COOKING TIME: 15 MINUTES SERVES: 2

Hugh Quarshie

A member of the Royal Shakespeare Company where he has played parts ranging from Marc Antony to Mephistopheles, actor Hugh Quarshie's diverse on screen roles include 'Star Wars Episode 1', 'Highlander' and 'Holby City'.

23

INGREDIENTS

1 tbsp oil • 2 cooked skinless chicken breasts, chopped • 125g garlic and herb full fat soft cheese • 2-3 tbsp milk • Seasoning • 250g pasta shapes such as fusilli or penne

QUICK GARLIC & HERB PASTA

For professional pasta-lovers with no time to prepare complicated dishes, this dish is seriously simple and seriously tasty.

1 Place a large pan of water on high heat and add a pinch of salt.

2 When it's bubbling rapidly pop in the pasta, being careful to separate it with a fork to prevent sticking. Cook until al dente (around 8 minutes)

3 In a large frying pan, warm the oil on medium heat. Add the chicken and stir fry until heated through.

4 Drain the pasta, except for a tablespoon of the water, and return to the pan. Add the chicken, half the cheese and the milk and stir until melted. Crumble the remaining cheese into the saucepan and toss. Cook, serve and eat immediately.

PREPARATION TIME: 5 MINUTES COOKING TIME: 10 MINUTES SERVES: 2

Jane Asher

As well as her many appearances in film and television, actress Jane Asher is now also well known as a writer and as one of Britain's leading cake makers. She is married to the cartoonist and illustrator Gerald Scarfe.

24

INGREDIENTS

25g dried porcini mushrooms • 25g butter • 2 tbsp olive oil • 1 onion, sliced • 100g thick sliced ham, chopped • Seasoning • 250g mushrooms, sliced • 150ml double cream • 50g Parmesan • 450g dried penne

PENNE WITH PORCINI & HAM

The full-flavoured porcini mushrooms give any dish a real depth and richness. With ham they make a glorious match, but the porcini are so meaty and succulent that this is a great veggie option without it.

1. Soak the dried porcini in boiling water for 8 minutes.

2. Place a large pot of water on high heat and add a pinch of salt.

3. When it's boiling rapidly add in the pasta, being careful to separate it with a fork to prevent sticking. Cook until al dente (around 8 minutes).

4. In a large frying pan warm the butter and oil on medium heat. Add the onion and cook gently until soft but not golden in colour. Add the ham and cook for 3 minutes more.

5. Drain the mushrooms, keeping the liquid. Finely chop the porcini and add to the onion and ham. Add the soaking liquid. Raise the heat and cook until all the water has evaporated. Add the sliced mushrooms and cook for 8 minutes or until all the water the mushrooms release has evaporated and they begin to brown.

6. Add the cream and cook until the cream has thickened and reduced. Remove from the heat.

7. Drain the pasta, and return to the pan. Add the mushroom sauce and toss gently. Serve and savour.

PREPARATION TIME: 15 MINUTES COOKING TIME: 20 MINUTES SERVES: 4

25

Marie Helvin

One of the world's most famous models, Marie's career has seen her grace the cover of 'British Vogue' 7 times and she has remained at the forefront of the fashion industry for over 30 years.

INGREDIENTS

2 tbsp olive oil • ½ onion, roughly chopped • 4 cloves garlic, crushed • 240g tinned chopped tomatoes • 1 tbsp tomato purée • Pinch caster sugar • 1 tsp vinegar • Pinch black pepper • Large handful basil leaves • 300g riccioli pasta

RICCIOLI LAST-MINUTE

Forgot to go to the supermarket? Scrape out your store cupboard and whip up this simple and tasty sauce.

1   First make the tomato sauce. In a large frying pan heat the oil on medium heat. Add the onions and fry gently for 2-3 minutes, then add the garlic and fry for a further 2-3 minutes, stirring often.

2   Pour in the tomatoes, tomato purée, sugar, vinegar, salt and freshly ground pepper and half the basil. Bring to the simmer then reduce the heat and cook gently for 6-7 minutes. Cool slightly, and then blend using a hand or jug blender.

3   Place a large pan of water on high heat and add a pinch of salt.

4   When it's bubbling rapidly pop in the pasta, being careful to separate it with a fork to prevent sticking. Cook until al dente (around 8 minutes).

5   Drain the pasta, except for 2 tbsp of the water, and return to the pan. Add the tomato sauce and stir gently before serving with a sprinkling of basil.

PREPARATION TIME: 10 MINUTES   COOKING TIME: 20 MINUTES   SERVES: 4

26

Martin Freeman

An accomplished actor of the stage and screen, Martin is probably best known for playing Arthur Dent in 'The Hitchhiker's Guide to the Galaxy' and his role as Tim Canterbury in Ricky Gervais & Stephen Merchant's 'The Office'.

INGREDIENTS

6 tbsp extra virgin olive oil • 2 cloves garlic, crushed • ½ tsp red chilli flakes • 300g scallops • 3 tbsp white wine • 2 tbsp breadcrumbs, lightly toasted • 2 tbsp freshly chopped parsley • Handful of rocket • Salt • 450g vermicelli

VERMICELLI WITH SCALLOPS

The genius of this dish is the breadcrumbs that soak up all the tasty flavour of the scallops and cling to the pasta. Tiger prawns work nicely as an alternative to the scallops.

1. Place a large pan of water on a high heat and add a pinch of salt.

2. When it's bubbling rapidly pop in the pasta, being careful to separate it with a fork to prevent sticking. Cook until al dente (around 8 minutes).

3. Heat 4 tbsp olive oil in a large pan, add the garlic and chilli flakes and cook over a medium-high heat until the garlic starts to sizzle. Add the scallops, raise the temperature to high and sear the scallops for 2 minutes on each side or until they have lost their translucency.

4. Pour in the wine, which should loosen the tasty bits from the bottom of the pan.

5. Drain the pasta, return to the pan and toss well with the contents. Add the remaining olive oil, breadcrumbs, parsley and rocket. Toss again and serve immediately.

PREPARATION TIME: 5 MINUTES COOKING TIME: 10 MINUTES SERVES: 4

VERMICELLI WITH SCALLOPS

Nicki Chapman

After working with artists such as the Spice Girls, Will Young and S Club 7 and judging both 'Popstars' and 'Pop Idol' Nicki has gone on to carve out a very successful career as a daytime television presenter.

27

INGREDIENTS

For the sauce: • 2 tbsp olive oil • 1 medium onion, chopped • 1 x 400g can chopped tomatoes with garlic • 125ml red wine • 125ml hot beef stock • ½ tsp brown sugar • 1 tbsp tomato purée • 1 tbsp basil

For the meatballs: • 100g breadcrumbs • 4 tbsp milk • 300g minced beef • 300g minced pork • 100g Parmesan cheese • Small handful chopped flat leaf parsley • 1 small onion, finely chopped • 1 clove garlic, finely chopped • 1 egg • ¼ tsp nutmeg • 400g spaghetti

SPAGHETTI & MEATBALLS

Sometimes dubbed as the 'Godfather of pasta dishes' you'd be hard pushed to find this Italian-American dish back in the Old Country. The secret to success here is the size of the meatballs — remember that a walnut is better than a golf ball!

1   For the sauce: Heat the oil in a large pan and cook the onion until soft. Stir in the tomatoes, wine, stock, sugar and tomato purée. Leave to simmer gently until the meatballs are ready to go in.

2   For the meatballs: soak the breadcrumbs in the milk for 10 minutes. Add the beef, pork, cheese, herbs, onion, garlic, egg and nutmeg. Season and mix together, breaking up any clumps of meat with a fork.

3   Roll the mixture into walnut-sized balls. Heat a little oil in a frying pan and fry the meatballs until brown and slightly crispy. Drain on kitchen paper.

4   Add the meatballs to the tomato sauce and cook for a further 15 minutes.

5   Place a large pan of water on high heat and add a pinch of salt.

6   When it's bubbling rapidly pop in the spaghetti, careful to separate it with a fork to prevent sticking. Cook until al dente (around 8 minutes).

7   Stir the basil through the sauce and serve tossed with the drained spaghetti — a dish you can't refuse.

PREPARATION TIME: 15 MINUTES   COOKING TIME: 25 MINUTES   SERVES: 4

28

Pattie Boyd

This model, photographer and muse was the inspiration for love songs written by both George Harrison (Something) and Eric Clapton (Layla, Wonderful Tonight & Bell Bottom Blues).

INGREDIENTS

50g butter • 50g plain flour, minus 1 tsp • 700ml full-fat milk, plus a bit extra • 175g mature Cheddar, grated • 50g Gruyère, grated • 1 rounded tsp Dijon mustard • 50g Parmesan, grated • 50g white breadcrumbs • 6 sun-blushed tomatoes, drained • 280g good-quality macaroni

MACARONI CHEESE

This dish has developed into a classic comfort option. Mix and match your cheese and use any leftovers from the fridge. Freshly-fried bacon bits provide an extra flavour punch.

1   Preheat the oven to 220°C/fan 200°C/425°F/Gas mark 7.

2   Place a large pan of water on high heat and add a pinch of salt.

3   When it's bubbling rapidly pop in the pasta, being careful to separate it with a fork to prevent sticking. Cook until al dente (around 8 minutes).

4   Melt the butter over a medium heat and, when foaming, add the flour. Stir well and cook for about 4 minutes. The mixture will be quite thick.

5   Gradually add the milk to the mixture, stirring constantly. Keep adding the milk slowly until it's all used up. Simmer for 5 minutes, stirring until silky smooth. Add the Cheddar, Gruyère and mustard. Stir again until melted and smooth. Turn off the heat.

6   Mix together the Parmesan and breadcrumbs. Add the cheese sauce to the drained pasta and mix thoroughly.

7   Place the macaroni cheese into a shallow ovenproof dish and sprinkle with the Parmesan breadcrumbs. Top with the tomatoes and bake until golden brown on top, about 15 minutes. Eat and relax.

PREPARATION TIME: 10 MINUTES   COOKING TIME: 15 MINUTES   SERVES: 4

29

Tess Daly

"As a mum, I find it very comforting to know that Great Ormond Street Hospital is there in case the worst happens. From the moment you walk in you are struck not only by the professionalism and warmth of the staff, but also that everything they do is focussed around children."

INGREDIENTS

5 tbsp olive oil • 75g mushrooms • 2 cans whole artichoke hearts, drained and cut into quarters • 10 sun-blushed tomatoes in oil, drained • 1 fresh green chilli chopped • 1 x 450g can chopped tomatoes • 6 fresh basil leaves, chopped • Salt and pepper, to season • 35g baby spinach leaves • 300g penne

PENNE POMODORO SECCHI

With juicy sun-blushed tomatoes you can almost taste the Mediterranean sun pouring onto the Calabrian landscape. This summery dish is dripping with southern passion and flavour.

1 Heat ½ the oil in a large pan, add the mushrooms, artichokes, sun-blushed tomatoes and chilli and cook for a few minutes. Add chopped tomatoes and bring to boil.

2 Add the remaining olive oil and season well with salt and pepper. Simmer the sauce for 8 to 10 minutes on low heat.

3 Place a large pan of water on high heat and add a pinch of salt.

4 When it's bubbling rapidly pop in the pasta, being careful to separate it with a fork to prevent sticking. Cook until al dente.

5 Toss the sauce with the drained pasta. Stir in with chopped basil and spinach.

6 Serve immediately in a warm serving dish and garnish with the remaining basil leaves.

PREPARATION TIME: 5 MINUTES   COOKING TIME: 15 MINUTES   SERVES: 2

Sir Ranulph Fiennes

According to the Guinness Book of World Records Ran, as he is known, is the world's greatest living adventurer. The first man to visit both the North and South Poles by surface means, he is also the first man to completely cross Antarctica on foot.

INGREDIENTS

50g butter • 1 tbsp olive oil • 1 small onion, finely diced • 1 x 400g can Italian tomatoes, chopped • ½ tsp dried oregano • Salt and freshly-ground black pepper • 250g large prawns, fresh or defrosted, chopped • 100g mozzarella • 2-3 fresh basil leaves • 20 large pasta shells

PASTA SHELLS STUFFED WITH PRAWNS IN TOMATO SAUCE

Prawns have never seemed quite as at home as they do in large pasta shells. Try stuffing these impressive shells with bolognese, spinach, or pretty much anything else for great results.

1   In a large frying pan warm the butter and oil on medium heat. Add the onion and cook for 8 minutes, careful not to let them colour!

2   Add the tomatoes and bring to the boil, stir in the oregano and season with salt and freshly ground pepper. Reduce the heat and simmer gently for 15 minutes until slightly reduced and thickened. Add the prawns and simmer for a further 5 minutes.

3   Rip the mozzarella into bite-size pieces and add half to the tomato sauce.

4   Place a large pan of water on high heat and add a pinch of salt.

5   When it's bubbling rapidly pop in the pasta, being careful to separate it with a fork to prevent sticking. Cook until al dente (around 10 minutes).

6   Preheat the grill to a medium heat.

7   Drain the pasta well, and with a teaspoon spoon the tomato and prawn mix into the shells and place in an oven-proof dish. Pour the rest of the sauce on top of the shells and sprinkle with the remaining mozzarella. Season and grill for 5-7 minutes or until the mozzarella is golden brown.

8   Serve with a sprinkle of basil.

PREPARATION TIME: 4 MINUTES   COOKING TIME: 20 MINUTES   SERVES: 4

30

26 Until the advent of tomato sauce, pasta, like most food, was eaten dry with the fingers. Many people believe that the liquid sauce demanded the use of a fork which helped change the way we eat all food today.

27 Pasta was not invented in Italy. The Chinese are on record as having eaten pasta as early as 5000 BC.

28 In the 13th century the Pope set quality standards for pasta.

"Everything you see I owe to spaghetti."
SOPHIA LOREN
29

30 The iconic pasta dish Fettuccine Alfredo was invented in 1914 by Italian chef Alfredo de Lelio. Legend has it that Alfredo invented it when his wife was pregnant and refused to eat anything else. The restaurant and the dish became famous when Mary Pickford and Douglas Fairbanks stopped in while on their honeymoon in 1927. They in turn served his dish when they returned to Hollywood.

31 Further proof that Marco Polo didn't bring pasta back to Italy is found in the will of Ponzio Baestone, a Genoan soldier dated 1279, 16 years before Marco Polo returned from China. In it he bequeathed "bariscella peina de macarone" — a small basket of macaroni.

32 Thomas Jefferson is credited with introducing macaroni to the United States which he came across in Naples, while serving as the U.S. Ambassador to France. He ordered a pasta-making machine to be sent back to the States.

33 During the Great Fire of London of 1666, Samuel Pepys buried his "Parmazan cheese, as well as (his) wine and some other things" in order to preserve them.

34

"No man is lonely eating spaghetti; it requires so much attention."
CHRISTOPHER MORLEY

35 Mussels are a rich source of iodine, protein, iron, copper and selenium, and a good source of calcium, vitamin B2 and niacin. They are also a source of zinc. Their collective noun is a cluster of mussels.

36 The earliest surviving olive oil amphorae date to 3500 BC while the production of olive is assumed to have started before 4000 BC.

37 In Naples the pasta makers sat on long benches and used their feet to mix and knead the dough. This displeased the King of Naples, Ferdinando II, who hired a leading engineer called Spadaccini to improve the procedure. The new system consisted of adding boiling water to freshly ground flour and a machine made of bronze to kneed the dough. Spadaccini also came up with the brilliant idea of using a four-pronged fork for eating pasta.

31

Ridley's striking visual style in films such as 'Alien', 'Blade Runner', 'Thelma & Louise' and 'Gladiator' has made him one of the most influential British filmmakers and one of the most internationally respected film directors.

INGREDIENTS

4 tbsp olive oil • 4 pork loin steaks, cooked and cut into strips • 10-12 fresh sage leaves, roughly chopped • 1 tbsp lemon juice • Salt and ground black pepper • 300g dry tagliatelle/fettuccine/pappardelle

TAGLIATELLE WITH PORK & SAGE

Nothing brings out the full juicy flavours of pork quite like sage. Use fettuccine or pappardelle to vary the width of your pasta ribbon experience.

1 Heat the oil in a pan over a medium heat. Add the pork and stir-fry for 3-4 minutes or until cooked. Add the sage, lemon juice and seasoning, to taste.

2 Place a large pan of water on high heat and add a pinch of salt.

3 When it's bubbling rapidly pop in the pasta, being careful to separate it with a fork to prevent sticking. Cook until al dente (around 8 minutes).

4 Drain the pasta, and return to the pan. Add the sage, butter and pork and toss gently before serving.

PREPARATION TIME: 5 MINUTES COOKING TIME: 15 MINUTES SERVES: 4

32

Chesney
Hawkes

Pop singer and songwriter most
famous for his huge hit 'The One And
Only'. Chesney has written songs for
artists including Al, Caprice, Tricky,
Jennifer Paige & Tears for Fears.

INGREDIENTS

50g butter • 250ml double cream • ¼ tsp grated nutmeg • Salt • Freshly ground black pepper • 100g Parmesan, grated • 300g dry egg fettuccine

FETTUCCINE ALFREDO

This dish is also known as Fettuccine alla Romano, or simply al burro e panna (with butter and cream).

1 Place a large pan of water on high heat and add a pinch of salt.

2 When it's bubbling rapidly pop in the pasta, being careful to separate it with a fork to prevent sticking. Cook until al dente (around 8 minutes).

3 Place the butter and cream in a small pan and heat until the butter has melted. Add the nutmeg and season with salt and pepper. Cook for 2 minutes or until the cream has reduced and started to thicken. Remove from the heat.

4 Pour the sauce over the drained pasta, stir in the Parmesan, and satisfy the craving!

PREPARATION TIME: 5 MINUTES COOKING TIME: 15 MINUTES SERVES: 4

FETTUCCINE ALFREDO

33

Russell Howard

Hot property in the comedy world, his three sold-out solo tours have cemented his reputation as one of the best live acts in the country.

INGREDIENTS

2 garlic cloves, crushed • 50g fresh basil leaves, reserving a few leaves for garnish • 2 tbsp toasted pine nuts • Seasoning • Tbsp extra virgin olive oil • 50g freshly-grated Parmesan • 75g ricotta • 3 cooked chicken breasts, cubed • 400g spaghetti or linguine

SPAGHETTI WITH CREAMY BASIL PESTO

The best way to make silky smooth pesto is the traditional way – with a pestle and mortar, adding the basil leaves one by one. Failing that, a little processor will do – but careful not to overwork the pesto.

1 Place the garlic, basil, pine nuts, seasoning and 5 tablespoons olive oil in a mini food processor and pulse until the mixture is smooth. Scoop the mix into a bowl and add the cheese and ricotta.

2 Place a large pan of water on high heat and add a pinch of salt.

3 When it's bubbling rapidly pop in the pasta, being careful to separate it with a fork to prevent sticking. Cook until al dente (around 8 minutes).

4 In a large frying pan warm the remaining oil on medium heat. Add the chicken and stir fry until heated through.

5 When the pasta is about halfway done add 2 tbsp of the pasta water to the pesto mix and mix well.

6 Mix the creamy pesto with the drained pasta and the cooked chicken and serve with pesto pride.

PREPARATION TIME: 10 MINUTES COOKING TIME: 15 MINUTES SERVES: 4

34

Sheila
Hancock OBE

"Great Ormond Street Hospital saved
my grandson's life."

INGREDIENTS

3 tbsp extra virgin olive oil • 1 clove garlic, crushed • Pinch of hot red chilli flakes • 600g fresh tomatoes, peeled and chopped • 2 skinless salmon fillets, cubed • 300ml double cream • 6-8 basil leaves • 450g farfalle

FARFALLE WITH FRESH SALMON

Meaning 'butterflies' in Italian, farfalle also resemble bowties, which gives a slight formal edge to this classy dish. A subtle rich cream sauce sets the salmon off nicely. To make with smoked salmon, add the fish at the very end of the cooking.

1 In a large frying pan warm the oil on medium heat. Add the garlic and chilli flakes and cook until the garlic is sizzling. Add the tomatoes and season well. Cook until all the liquid has been released – this should take about 10-12 minutes.

2 Place a large pan of water on high heat and add a pinch of salt.

3 When it's bubbling rapidly pop in the pasta, being careful to separate it with a fork to prevent sticking. Cook until al dente (around 8 minutes).

4 Add the salmon to the tomatoes and stir in the cream. Cook until the cream has thickened and salmon cooked. Add shredded basil.

5 When the pasta is cooked, drain and add the salmon and tomato sauce. Serve at once.

PREPARATION TIME: 5 MINUTES COOKING TIME: 10 MINUTES SERVES: 4

FARFALLE WITH
FRESH SALMON

Stephen Merchant

Co-writer and co-director of the multi-award winning 'The Office' and 'Extras', Stephen is much in demand as a writer, broadcaster, comedian and actor.

35

INGREDIENTS

6 tbsp extra virgin olive oil • 1 clove garlic, crushed • Large handful flat leaf parsley • 2 sprigs of rosemary • 2 sprigs of thyme • Salt • 7-8 basil leaves • 3 tbsp breadcrumbs • 600g vermicelli

VERMICELLI WITH FRESH HERBS

Rosemary and thyme make this dish intensely aromatic and the parsley and basil round off the flavours. The breadcrumbs not only soak up all the delicious juices but give an additional crunch.

1 Place a large pan of water on high heat and add a pinch of salt.

2 When it's bubbling rapidly pop in the pasta, being careful to separate it with a fork to prevent sticking. Cook until al dente (around 8 minutes).

3 In a large frying pan warm the oil on medium heat. Add the garlic and parsley and cook until the garlic is sizzling. Add the rosemary and thyme. Season, add the shredded basil and cook for a further 30 seconds.

4 Drain the pasta, and add the sauce and breadcrumbs and toss gently.

PREPARATION TIME: 5 MINUTES COOKING TIME: 10 MINUTES SERVES: 4

Vernon
Kay

36

Aside from his 'day job' as a radio and television presenter Vernon is also a Patron of Great Ormond Street Hospital Children's Charity and alongside his wife, Tess Daly, has become actively involved in supporting the hospital.

INGREDIENTS

2 tbsps olive oil • 100g pancetta • 175g button mushrooms, quartered • 2 garlic cloves, finely chopped • 250ml single cream • 3 spring onions, chopped • 2 tbsp of peas • 1 tbsp fresh chopped flat leaf parsley • 300g spaghetti

SPAGHETTI BOSCAIOLA

Boscaiola means 'woodman's style', a perfect dish after a hard day's foraging.

1 Heat oil in the pan and cook the pancetta until crispy and brown. Add the mushrooms and cook together with the pancetta. Add chopped garlic and cook until it starts to brown.

2 Stir in the cream on low heat and simmer for 5-8 minutes until the sauce starts to thicken.

3 Add the spring onion and peas, and cook for a further 5 minutes.

4 Place a large pan of water on high heat and add a pinch of salt.

5 When it's bubbling rapidly pop in the pasta, being careful to separate it with a fork to prevent sticking. Cook until al dente.

6 Gently stir the sauce with the drained pasta, serve immediately in a warm serving dish and garnish with chopped parsley.

PREPARATION TIME: 5 MINUTES COOKING TIME: 15 MINUTES SERVES: 2

37

Robert &
Babs Powell

As an actor Robert's roles have included Jesus of Nazareth and Robert Hannay. Former 'Pan's People' Babs is an amateur yachtswoman who holds the record of being the oldest housewife to visit both the North and South Poles.

INGREDIENTS

6 tbsp extra virgin olive oil • 6-7 basil leaves, shredded • 125g prosciutto • 3 tbsp black olives, sliced • Chunk of Parmesan, for shaving • Seasoning • 350g fusilli pasta

FUSILLI WITH PROSCIUTTO & BASIL OIL

Ensure you use good quality prosciutto and fresh aromatic basil here – as ingredient quality is paramount in this simple dish.

1 Pour the olive oil into a small saucepan and heat gently. Add the basil leaves, remove from the heat and leave to infuse for 30 minutes.

2 In a large frying pan warm the basil oil on medium heat. Add the prosciutto and cook for a minute or two or until crispy. Add the olives and toss gently.

3 Place a large pan of water on high heat and add a pinch of salt.

4 When it's bubbling rapidly pop in the pasta, being careful to separate it with a fork to prevent sticking. Cook until al dente (around 8 minutes).

5 Drain the pasta and return to the pan. Add the contents of the other pan, season and toss gently. Serve immediately with a few Parmesan shavings – again, the better the Parmesan, the better the end product!

PREPARATION TIME: 10 MINUTES PLUS 30 MINUTES INFUSION
COOKING TIME: 10 MINUTES SERVES: 4

38

Tamzin Outhwaite

Since her award winning role as Mel in 'Eastenders', Tamzin has starred in numerous shows on stage and screen including 'Hotel Babylon', 'The Fixer', 'Red Cap' and 'Paradox'. She is delighted to once again support Great Ormond Street Hospital Children's Charity.

INGREDIENTS

1 slice white bread, crust removed • 50ml milk • 1 garlic clove, crushed • 125g shelled walnuts • 1 tsp fresh chopped oregano plus leave to garnish • 3 tbsp extra virgin olive oil • 450g linguine

LINGUINE WITH WALNUT PESTO

In Liguria, the Italian Riviera, walnut pesto is nearly as popular as basil pesto. This dish is also delicious with a crumbling of Gorgonzola just before serving.

1 Place the bread in a small bowl, pour over the milk and leave to soak for 10 minutes.

2 Place the garlic, walnuts, oregano and olive oil into a small food processor. Add the bread and milk and season. Pulse to a creamy consistency.

3 Place a large pan of water on high heat and add a pinch of salt.

4 When it's bubbling rapidly pop in the pasta, being careful to separate it with a fork to prevent sticking. Cook until al dente (around 8 minutes).

5 Add 2 tbsp of the pasta water to the walnut pesto and mix thoroughly. Drain the pasta and return to the pan. Add the pesto, toss and serve garnished with a few fresh oregano leaves.

PREPARATION TIME: 10 MINUTES COOKING TIME: 10 MINUTES SERVES: 4

LINGUINE WITH WALNUT PESTO

INGREDIENTS

3 tbsp extra virgin olive oil • 1 clove garlic, chopped • 1 tbsp fresh chopped flat leaf parsley, plus extra for garnish • Pinch red chilli flakes • 100ml dry white wine • 450g ripe tomatoes, peeled and roughly chopped • 700g fresh live mussels, washed and de-bearded • Seasoning • 8-10 basil leaves • 450g spaghetti

SPAGHETTI WITH MUSSELS

This bracing marine dish should transport you to your favourite seaside town. Enjoy with plenty of crusty bread to soak up all the tasty juices.

1 Place the oil, garlic, parsley and chilli flakes in a large pan. Heat over a medium heat for about 15 seconds or until the garlic sizzles. Pour in the wine and let bubble for a minute. Add the tomatoes and season. Cook until the tomatoes break down into a sauce, this should take about 3 minutes.

2 Place a large pan of water on high heat and add a pinch of salt.

3 When it's bubbling rapidly pop in the pasta, being careful to separate it with a fork to prevent sticking. Cook until al dente (around 8 minutes).

4 Add the mussels to the tomato sauce, cover and cook until the mussels have opened — about 3-4 minutes. Discard any mussels that do not open. Remove from heat.

5 When the pasta is ready, drain well and put into pan with mussels and sauce. Toss gently over a very low heat so the flavours combine.

6 Serve at once with a sprinkling of chopped parsley.

PREPARATION TIME: 5 MINUTES COOKING TIME: 10 MINUTES SERVES: 4

Brian Turner CBE

Brian Turner is one of Britain's most respected and best known chefs appearing regularly on 'Ready Steady Cook' and 'This Morning', 'Saturday Cooks' and 'Saturday Kitchen'.

40

INGREDIENTS

450g fresh ripe tomatoes, peeled and seeds removed • 1 yellow pepper, de-seeded and finely chopped • 1 red chilli, de-seeded and finely chopped • 3 tbsp fresh chopped flat leaf parsley • 2 tbsp extra virgin olive oil • 100g pancetta cubes • Seasoning • 450g rigatoni

RIGATONI WITH PEPPER, BACON & TOMATO SAUCE

These ridged tubes are ideal for picking up tomato-based sauces — and the key to this fine summer dish is the ripest, most fragrant tomatoes you can find.

1 Place the tomatoes, pepper, chilli and parsley and a light grinding of black pepper into a food processor and pulse into a purée.

2 Place a large pan of water on high heat and add a pinch of salt.

3 When it's bubbling rapidly pop in the pasta, being careful to separate it with a fork to prevent sticking. Cook until al dente (around 8 minutes).

4 Heat the oil in a small frying pan. Add the pancetta and fry until golden brown. Add to the tomatoes and stir.

5 Drain the pasta and return to the pan. Add the tomato sauce and leave to stand for a couple of minutes. Serve and enjoy.

PREPARATION TIME: 10 MINUTES COOKING TIME: 10 MINUTES SERVES: 4

**Great
Ormond
Street
Hospital**
Charity

Great Ormond Street Hospital is one of the world's leading children's hospitals. The hospital first opened its doors on the 14th February 1852 with ten beds and quickly attracted public support. Queen Victoria, Charles Dickens and JM Barrie, who donated the copyright to his famous play Peter Pan, were among the first to pledge their help.

Today it receives more than 200,000 patient visits every year from children from all over the world. In the UK, the hospital has the largest range of children's specialists under one roof. Many of the children the hospital treats have complex and unique conditions that require the expertise that only Great Ormond Street Hospital can provide. The hospital has the largest children's cancer unit in Europe, the largest centre for children's heart transplants worldwide and also boasts the largest centre for research into paediatric illness outside of the US.

Whilst the NHS meets the day to day running costs of the hospital, fundraising income is essential for Great Ormond Street Hospital to remain at the forefront of child healthcare. The current priority for Great Ormond Street Hospital Children's Charity is to fund the essential redevelopment of two thirds of the hospital, parts of which were built in the 1930's. As paediatric medicine advances, the buildings have become out dated and unfit for purpose; they are simply too cramped for our growing needs. As well as funding the redevelopment, the charity continues to support other aspects of the hospital's work, such as research grants, parent's accommodation and specialist medical equipment.

To find out more about the amazing work that Great Ormond Street Hospital does, visit www.gosh.org.

ASK is once again delighted to support Great Ormond Street Hospital Children's Charity as part of its ongoing commitment to the charity which will make a real difference to the lives of the patients and their families.

The donations from these books and the ongoing Great Ormond Street Hospital Children's Charity fundraising activity from ASK will be used to build a new ward kitchen urgently needed at the hospital. Prior to the commencement of this activity ASK has already guaranteed a minimum donation of £35,000.

These books will be available at all ASK restaurants. ASK will be running promotions in all its restaurants throughout the year in support of Great Ormond Street Hospital Children's Charity.

To find your nearest ASK restaurant go to www.askrestaurants.com